"Rohingya people who are living in Myanmar don't have rights. Even a bird has rights. A bird can build a nest, give birth, bring food to their children and raise them until they are ready to fly. We don't have basic rights like this."

Exiled to Nowhere
BURMA'S ROHINGYA

~

Greg Constantine

Foreword by Emma Larkin

The Burmese authorities take photos of Rohingya families so they know exactly how many people live in each household. The slightest discrepancy to the family register often results in heavy fines and punishment.

Stripped of their Burmese citizenship in 1982 and deprived of most social, economic and civil rights, many Rohingya feel they have no option but to leave Burma. These women fled Burma in early 2009.

Over the past twenty years, many Rohingya have fled their homeland and now live as unrecognized refugees in neighboring Bangladesh. Thousands live in squalid makeshift refugee camps.

FOREWORD

Emma Larkin
April 2012
Bangkok, Thailand

"We Rohingya are like orchids," an 18-year-old Rohingya man called Shamsul once told me. "We are not able to grow any roots in the ground so we are left with only one way to stay alive and that is to cling on to others."

At the time I met Shamsul, in 2008, he was living with around 10,000 other Rohingya refugees in a makeshift camp wedged along a narrow strip of land between a busy highway and the muddy banks of the Naf River, which marks the divide between Burma and Bangladesh. Located on the Bangladesh side of the river, the camp was a conglomeration of wretched hovels cobbled together from twigs and salvaged scraps; the space between each hut was barely wide enough for a single person to walk through. Hordes of ragged children stampeded along the narrow dirt pathways playing with bits of rubbish—an empty cigarette packet, a condom blown-up like a balloon. The refugees living there survived hand-to-mouth; men picked up day-labor jobs at the port, others risked beatings and jail-sentences to forage for firewood in the forest, and women went to the nearby town of Teknaf to beg.

Shamsul's lifetime ambition was to become a driver for the commuter buses he saw barreling along the highway each day but it was an unrealizable dream; to get a driving license he would need a Bangladesh identity card and, for the Rohingya, that was virtually impossible. Spurned in Burma and barely tolerated by the Bangladeshi government, these Rohingya were stuck in limbo, both stateless and homeless. Indeed, the camp had the claustrophobic, stagnant air of a dead end.

It was, for me, a powerful indictment of just how bad conditions must be for Rohingya living in Burma that they would willingly put themselves in this hopeless position.

For nearly half a century, Burma was ruled by a military dictatorship that had one of the worst records for human rights abuses in the world. The borders of modern-day Burma were drawn around eight different ethnic groups (of which the Burmese are by far the largest) and, since independence from the British colonial government in 1948, the Burmese army has been engaged in violent conflicts against numerous ethnic forces fighting for freedom or increased autonomy. To flush out guerilla fighters, Burmese soldiers razed whole villages, commandeered civilians as army porters and human minesweepers and, in some regions, practiced systematic rape of ethnic women. Meanwhile, in other areas of the country, a vast network of spies and informers ensured that anyone who did or said anything that might threaten the regime would be swiftly identified and punished. A meticulous censorship board prevented anti-government sentiment from sneaking into print—all books, magazines, movie scripts, and song lyrics had to be approved by the censors before printing. The authorities also churned out clumsy propaganda that ranged in style from the ominous red billboards ("Crush all Those Harming the Union") to state newspapers like the New Light of Myanmar, which published daily pictures of the ruling generals engaged in benign activities such as overseeing the opening of new schools or bridges and paying reverential visits to Buddhist pagodas. Anyone who disagreed with this rarified version of events and dared to speak it out loud risked torture and imprisonment. It was, in short, a very Orwellian state.

While life in Burma is tough for most people who live there it is especially hard on the Rohingya, who are among the most beleaguered minorities in the world. Though they trace their origins back to Arab traders who arrived in northwestern Burma as early as the 9th century, the Burmese government does not recognize them as one of the country's 135 indigenous races and they are not allowed to take on Burmese citizenship. As a result, they are restricted from marrying or owning land. They cannot travel beyond their own villages or enroll their children in formal education. Over the past decades hundreds of thousands of Rohingya have fled to Bangladesh, bringing with them accounts of forced labor, rape, torture and summary executions at the hands of the Burmese army. Largely ignored by the international community, denied a home in Burma or a true sanctuary in Bangladesh, the Rohingya refugees are considered illegal immigrants in both countries and remain, as Shamsul described them, unable to grow any roots.

As this book goes to press, the news coming from Burma has been—for the first time in many, many years—astonishingly positive. A general election has taken place, new political parties have been formed, and a nominally civilian government is in power. The long political stalemate appears to be coming to an end as Burma's Nobel Peace Laureate and democracy leader, Aung San Suu Kyi, participated in this year's by-elections and prepares to enter government. Ceasefires have been brokered in various ethnic states. The draconian censorship rules are easing and the media is being afforded more freedom. Yet, so far, these seemingly positive changes have had few ramifications for the Rohingya and it is still uncertain whether they will have any valid voice in the new parliament. While other taboo topics can now be covered in the local Burmese media, any reporting on Rohingya issues is still banned. In Burma, at least, their story remains under wraps.

The pages that follow are a rare documentation of the plight of the Rohingya. Guided by the voices of the Rohingya themselves, Greg Constantine has pieced together an epic and intimate tale of a people who, quite literally, have nowhere to go.

VOICES

Tomás Ojea Quintana
UN Special Rapporteur on Human Rights in Myanmar

The Rohingya are definitely people from Myanmar. They were born in Myanmar, have lived in Myanmar together with other ethnic groups for centuries, have participated in the political and cultural history of Myanmar, have suffered the same oppression and human rights abuses as many others in Myanmar, and now deserve an active participation at this unique opportunity to build peace, democracy and respect for fundamental rights.

As the United Nations Human Rights Special Rapporteur I visited the country five times. Once to Northern Rakhine State in 2010, including Sittwe and Buthidaung. I met Rohingya in their own land, and I saw a strong ethnic community living its life amid fear and oppression. Throughout my mandate, I also interviewed Rohingya who had to flee, and I heard awful stories about human rights abuses. Thanks to the tireless commitment of NGOs, journalists, academics, researchers, UN States, and Rohingyas fighting for their community, the cause of this ethnic minority has always been alive.

Now, after decades of oppression and endemic discrimination against the Rohingya, I believe there is an opportunity to work for a real change. The new Government faces many and complex issues, but the cause of Rohingyas must be a priority. We have to work for this.

David Scott Mathieson
Senior Researcher on Burma
Human Rights Watch

The Rohingya of Burma have for decades been stranded at the outer reaches of international mercy and assistance. Their internal exile by the Burmese state has produced the most deplorable humanitarian, human rights and stateless situations in a country that has long endured a dismal blend of autocracy, repression and poverty. Using bureaucratic authoritarianism and brute force, petty rules limiting freedoms of movement, right to work, ability to marry, and restrictions on religious expression alongside routine and racist violence, the Burmese authorities make life so miserable, flight often becomes the only option. Rohingya refugees fleeing to Bangladesh have fared little better, as they are confined to camps or scrape a living as frequently abused migrant workers. This cross-border repression has sparked a steady stream of Rohingya seeking work in Southeast Asia, often after perilous journeys by boat. There are few if any comparable cases of regionalized human rights disasters as that faced by the Rohingya.

After ten years covering human rights in Burma, the Rohingya for me always looms the darkest and most intractable of a miserable landscape. Rendering clear the human dimension of protracted statelessness, Greg Constantine has granted the Rohingya a basic right Burma and communities refuse to grant, and the international community is incapable of improving: basic human dignity.

Michel Gabaudan
President
Refugees International

"Ugly as ogres" is how one Burmese diplomat publicly described the Rohingya. "Illegal residents" is how they are officially identified inside the country. Both characterizations are wrong, but after decades of forceful repetition they have hardened the minds of Burma's leaders and its people. Outside Burma, many nations are on record condemning the marginalization and persecution of the Rohingya as one of the world's most extreme violations of human rights. Now, however, as these same countries work furiously to hasten Burma's fragile reforms, they have conveniently forgotten their past concern for the Rohingya—no doubt in an attempt to placate Burma's new leaders and advance their own national interests.

Every day Rohingya flee Burma, humiliated and paralyzed by policies that leave them desperate to find work and sanctuary in Bangladesh and elsewhere, yet they are often grossly neglected or forced back. No one decries these violations when the victims are the Rohingya.

For decades, global leaders have told us the time is not right to address the Rohingya in a meaningful way. In reality, however, there is no right time. Unless the world intervenes, they will always be considered pariahs at home, victims abroad, and damned either way.

Harn Yawnghwe
Executive Director
Euro-Burma Office, Brussels

Democracy and human rights, applies to all peoples: Burmans, Shans, Pa-O, Palaung, Wa, Kokang, Karens, Rohingyas and others. I was shocked when my colleagues in the Burmese democracy movement reacted strongly and emotionally at the mention of the word "Rohingya". There is a deep fear amongst the Buddhist Rakhines that the Muslim Rohingyas will take over their ancestral homeland. They, therefore, object strongly to the word "Rohingya" and in the process try to deny their very existence. The Rohingya are human beings and must be accorded basic human rights. They have lived in Burma for at least a hundred years, if not more. Should they not be citizens and accorded citizenship rights as well? If we want democracy in Burma, should they also not be accorded political rights?

As to the question of the Rohingyas legal status, this is a political issue that needs to be resolved politically. Denying the Rohingya the right to call themselves Rohingyas is not the right solution. Suppressing them, restricting them, abusing them, insulting them and excluding them, will not solve the problem. To build a sustainable democracy in Burma, we must be inclusive, and we must respect each other. Otherwise, the democracy we dream of will never be achieved.

Benjamin Zawacki
Myanmar Researcher
Amnesty International

The Rohingya represent a classic example of how making an issue everyone's responsibility results in it being no one's at all: There is wide agreement among at least six South and/or Southeast Asian countries that a "regional solution" to the "Rohingya problem" must be found, but no country has been willing to assume any kind of leadership.

It begins, and could quite simply end, in Myanmar, where over a million Rohingya live, and from which hundreds or more flee each year. Most travel by land to Bangladesh (where they are only slightly less unwelcome but blend in far easier), others by sea to Malaysia, southern Thailand, even Indonesia. Those who survive the journey—Thai security forces have a record of detaining, beating, and/or "pushing back" boatloads of Rohingyas without food, water, or fuel—tell harrowing tales of systemic discrimination and persecution in Myanmar. The Burmese deny them citizenship, severely restrict their right to marry, the opportunity to work for the government, and their freedom of movement. So many leave—leaving the region, and themselves, no closer to a durable solution.

António Guterres
UN High Commissioner for Refugees

The Muslims of northern Rakhine State, often known as Rohingya, are people the UN refugee agency cares deeply about. At the request of the Myanmar government, UNHCR is working to make life better for them and the Rakhine community. We hope the reconciliation process now underway in Myanmar will pay benefits for them. We believe that as they come to enjoy better rights, better legal status and a living wage inside northern Rakhine State, they will have less reason to risk their lives in unseaworthy boats looking for asylum or menial work in other countries.

We are also working with countries in the region to improve life for Rohingya in exile. We are pressing for their rights first of all to seek and receive refugee status, and to get identity documents, registration, legal residence, and the right to work. With these rights should come health care and education. Our goal is for countries in the region to co-operate on protecting the Rohingya, and work with Myanmar to improve conditions inside northern Rakhine State.

Aryeh Neier
President
Open Society Foundations

As I write, reports on the political opening underway in Burma are heartening and exciting. They reawaken hope that even a dictatorship that is seemingly impervious to change can be transformed. Yet it is not yet evident that the changes now taking place will make a difference for those in Burma who have been the most marginalized of all and whose suffering has never attracted significant international attention: the Rohingya. They have been severely abused by the Burmese authorities and also by other governments when they have sought refuge elsewhere. By bringing us face to face with the Rohingya through his photographs, Greg Constantine is making it possible for the world to get to know the Rohingya and to try to see to it that the opening in Burma extends to them. They require recognition as citizens of Burma or Myanmar. Indeed, they require recognition of their right to have rights.

Chris Lewa
The Arakan Project

The Rohingya are often portrayed as highly disempowered people—and in so many ways they are, deprived of rights and facing relentless hostility in almost every place they find themselves. However, their resilience amid such extreme deprivations is outstanding. In North Arakan, they may be beaten, extorted, imprisoned and denied most basic services but, day after day, they continue to find ways to survive in the land they and their ancestors have lived in for many generations.

As refugees, they show extraordinary skills of adaptation. Mostly illiterate, they acquire new languages and blend in with local culture wherever they go. Stateless and undocumented, they move with remarkable fluidity across borders as they seek a space to improve their lives. Their journey by boat illustrates acutely both their desperation but also their determination to survive on this earth against all odds. Any country willing to extend recognition and basic rights to the Rohingya, especially their native land of Myanmar, would benefit enormously from a people with such energy and strength.

"The Rohingya are people split by a border. People on both sides look the same. They have the same religion. Speak the same language. Have the same color. The same culture. They have the same face. In Burma we are accused of being Bangladeshi and because of that, they torture us."

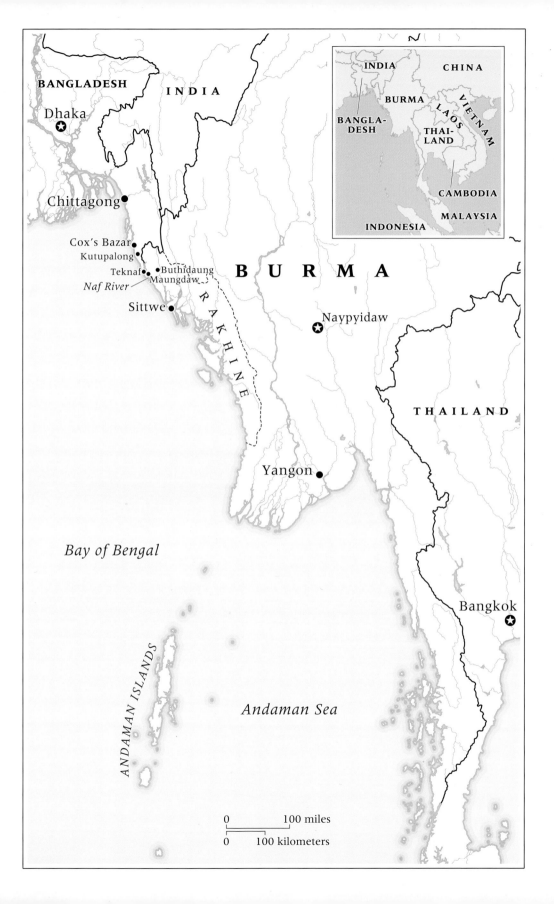

PART ONE

"Since we don't have nationality in Burma, we can't live in peace. In Burma they say we are from Bangladesh. When we come to Bangladesh, they say we are from Burma. People view us as if we don't exist."

After being beaten in the head during forced labor in Burma, this man fled to Bangladesh in 1992. He is one of an estimated 300,000 unrecognized Rohingya refugees currently living in southern Bangladesh.

Jafar

"I was born in Buthidaung on Feb 22, 1978, the same month *Naga Min* started," 34-year-old Jafar says. A man selling deep-fried snacks walks by the tiny stall where Jafar and several other men sit. Across the dirt path, the distorted soundtrack of a Hindi movie can be heard coming through the gaps in the wood-planked walls of a small tea-shack-turned-movie-hall during the hotter parts of the afternoon. "I've lived more than half of my life as a refugee here in Bangladesh with no country to belong to," Jafar continues. "I was only days old when *Naga Min* started and we were unable to leave. Most of the people in my village fled to Bangladesh during *Naga Min*. Most of those same people were repatriated back to Burma, but still, none of us have been given nationality."

In early February 1978, Burma's military junta led by General Ne Win launched *Operation Naga Min* or Operation Dragon King. The punitive operation began in the Rakhine State of western Burma, historically known as Arakan, which is located near the border with Bangladesh. While the Rohingya had lived in Arakan for generations, the Ne Win government claimed most of the Muslims in Arakan had illegally migrated to Burma from the Chittagong area of Bangladesh, and since coming to power in 1962, Ne Win was gradually setting the stage to drive them out.

With the aim of purging Burma of illegal foreigners, *Naga Min* scrutinized the identity papers of people throughout Burma, especially those along the border regions. Yet, nowhere in Burma was *Naga Min* executed with as much ferocity than in Rakhine. In Rakhine, teams of immigration officials swept through villages, going house to house demanding identification papers, questioning documentation and swiftly punishing and arresting those who didn't meet up to the arbitrary requirements of those in charge. *Naga Min* sent a wave of terror throughout the Rohingya community in Rakhine, particularly the townships of Maungdaw, Buthidaung and Rathidaung in North Rakhine. It resulted in mass arrests as well as violence and widespread human rights abuse against Rohingya throughout Rakhine. Ultimately, *Naga Min* sparked an exodus of 250,000 Rohingya out of Burma into neighboring Bangladesh.

Under pressure from the international community, the Rohingya were forced back to Burma in 1979 in a repatriation agreement between Burma and Bangladesh. Less than three years later, Ne Win and the Burmese government enacted the 1982 Burma Citizenship Law, which created three categories of citizens. In practice the Law provides 'full' citizenship only to those from Burma's 135 recognized 'national races.' This list conspicuously omits the Rohingya, a minority over 800,000 strong, effectively making them a stateless people.

In 1991, five months after Jafar's thirteenth birthday, the events of *Naga Min* replayed themselves again, this time through *Operation Pyi Thaya* or Operation Clean and Beautiful Nation.

"People all over my village were being harassed," Jafar remembers.

Pyi Thaya unleashed another wave of widespread abuse, forced labor, harassment, rape, arbitrary land seizure and destruction of property across Rakhine. By the middle of 1992, another 250,000 Rohingya had crossed the Naf River again into southern Bangladesh, including Jafar and his family.

"It took us three days to get to Bangladesh," Jafar says. "We walked for one full day and slept in the forest. Then walked another day until we reached the coast where we slept in a forest next to the river. Then my father hired a small canoe. It took four hours for us to cross the Naf River and reach Teknaf. I asked my father, *Why can't we stay? We have cows. We have land. Why can't we stay and live on our land?* He told me, *We have no rights in Burma so it is time for us to leave. We must leave now.*"

Over the next few years, some 200,000 Rohingya would be returned to Burma through a UNHCR monitored repatriation program. Ultimately, thousands of unrecognized Rohingya, like Jafar and his family would remain in Bangladesh, convinced that life in Burma was unlivable. Today, twenty years later, 30,000 officially recognized refugees remain in two refugee camps, yet it is estimated that up to 300,000 unrecognized Rohingya refugees currently live throughout southern Bangladesh.

Even now, year after year, thousands more continue to slowly trickle out of Burma into Bangladesh, primarily to escape from the abuse they face at the hands of the special border security force created in 1992 called *Nay-Sat Kut-kwey Ye* or *NaSaKa*. Found only in North Rakhine and consisting of a conglomeration of police, immigration, customs, military intelligence, and anti-riot police, *NaSaKa* continues to be the main perpetrators of human rights abuse against the Rohingya in Burma, denying Rohingya the ability to travel freely, imposing strict restrictions on their right to get married, subjecting them to religious persecution, forced labor and arbitrary land seizure, and paralyzing them financially with excessive taxes, bribes and extortion.

While those who have left Burma yearn for the day they can return to their homeland, most Rohingya say their return will only come when they are provided the fundamental right they've been denied the past thirty years: citizenship.

"Myanmar is my home and that is where I want to go back to," Jafar says. "But none of us have citizenship and because we don't have citizenship we are like a fish out of water, flapping and unable to breathe. If we were to get citizenship in Burma, we would be like the fish that you catch and then throw back into the water where he belongs. But we can't do anything right now. We are still that fish out of water and when a fish is out of water, he suffocates to death. We have been out of water for such a long time and we are suffocating. We are suffocating to death right now."

"As Muslims we should be permitted to build mosques and madrassas in Arakan but it is not allowed.

If you build a mosque, they arrest you and put you in jail."

"We worked on the border fence for one month. We had to dig and make a road in the middle of the river. Every day we had to work. After finishing our work they never paid us.

Rohingya who live in Myanmar are still forced to work this way."

"When a Rohingya dies in Burma, we have to pay a tax. When a Rohingya is born in Burma, we are taxed. When a calf is born in Burma, we have to pay a tax. And when a cow dies in Burma we have to pay a tax."

"I'm from Maungdaw and one day the army came to our house in the middle of the afternoon and told my family that we had to leave. They gave no reason. They just said, 'This is not your land. You have to leave. This is our land.' My family had lived on that land for fifty years. I was born on that land. My father grew up on that land. It was our family land and working that land was the only way my family could earn money. We were paid nothing. They gave us nothing for the land we had lived on all those years.

After we left the land, I became very sick and fled to Bangladesh. I heard that NaSaKa removed my name from the family list, so there is no way I can return. Burma is my home country and I miss my country very much.

My land was given to Buddhist people. Now the land is owned by Buddhists but they are using Rohingya people to work the land."

"In Burma we are forced to build roads. We are forced to build jetties and piers and we are forced to build military camps and move all of the military equipment. We are forced to work sentry duty at night. If we doze off from exhaustion we are beaten. When we wake up we are beaten. And when we are beaten we are made to give away a chicken to pay for our punishment. My father was a farmer and had some land but it was confiscated by the military to build a military camp. I can remember working in the fields with my father.

When they confiscated our land we cried, but we had no way to say anything."

"I grew up in the country, outside of Sittwe, far away from North Arakan. After both of my parents died, the military came and said 'This is not your land so you have to go'. They put us on boats. There were five boats loaded with Rohingya, and the military took us up the river to Maungdaw in North Arakan. When we got to Maungdaw they put one family here; one family there, another family somewhere else. It was a totally unknown place to us. They gave us a hut for the twelve people in my family to live. We couldn't find work because we didn't have any land and we couldn't travel. The military came and took the land again and gave it to Buddhists to live on. We had nowhere to go, so we had to leave."

Fatima

A late afternoon rain has come and gone. The breeze has died and the sun breaks through a large opening in the clouds. Everything immediately seems to slow down from the humidity. From inside Fatima's hut, the faint voice of the afternoon call to prayer can be heard. No loudspeaker. Just a tired set of vocal chords. Almost one year has passed since Fatima and her husband, Nazir, fled to Bangladesh. Four years ago, their families arranged for the two to marry. In her heart and in the eyes of God, Fatima and Nazir were married for several years, but not in the eyes of *NaSaKa*.

"If we want to marry in Burma, then we have to get permission from *NaSaKa*," Fatima says. Beads of sweat start to form on her forehead and upper lip. "They said that we had to provide them with photographs and pay them money. So we paid, but then they said there was a problem with our photos and made us give them more photos and charged us more money. We waited one and a half years, but they never gave us permission."

"While we were waiting, we got married according to Islamic law, not officially by the government, and I got pregnant. Everybody knew I was pregnant. When *NaSaKa* found out we were married in secret, we were called to their office and they demanded more money."

Fatima's friend, 20-year-old Amina, sits next to her. Amina has already shared her story, saying most Rohingya their age had, in one form or another, experienced the same thing. And she was right. Not far from Fatima's hut there's 26-year-old Hossina, who never received marriage permission. And 24-year-old Gul, who waited years. And 18-year-old Arefa whose parents spent almost everything they had to get marriage permission for their daughter, which was never granted. And 30-year-old Abdul, who waited three years and then—after finding out that *NaSaKa* wanted to arrest him because he and his bride got married in a secret Islamic ceremony—had no choice but to flee to Bangladesh to evade arrest.

All were subject to the same form of persecution imposed by a single document. In 1994, the Burmese authorities issued a Local Order that required Rohingya wishing to marry to first receive formal permission from *NaSaKa*. The Order was issued in North Rakhine only and nowhere else in the country. Marriages conducted without prior permission are illegal. Those who disobey the order, especially men, can be arrested and prosecuted under Section 493 of the Penal Code, which can carry a sentence of up to 10 years.

Couples (and their families) must usually pay enormous amounts in extortion money and often have to wait years for permission to be granted. They must also sign a statement claiming they will have no more than two children. It is very common for a pregnancy test to be conducted before permission is granted.

As a result, young Rohingya like Hossina, Gul and Fatima often have no choice but to submit to the humiliation and severe consequences involved throughout the entire process. They see it as yet another administrative tactic for the Burmese authorities to systematically discriminate against them, extort money from them, and add on another stressful and degrading element of control and fear over their lives, with the ultimate goal to push them out of the country.

Fatima continues. "First they demanded money from my husband's parents, then, they demanded money from my parents. My parents didn't have the money so we paid them by giving them our cattle and land. Then the officials told me, *You have to have an abortion, otherwise we will send you to prison*. I had no choice. So, I got the abortion."

"When I got the abortion the officials told me that my husband and I still needed to get permission to be married. We waited another one and a half years but I got pregnant again. That time the officials demanded more money than before. They said, *Why are you committing all of these crimes?* That time I was five months pregnant. A village doctor helped me. He gave me an injection. A local midwife helped me give birth to the dead baby. Both abortions were done this way.

"My husband was put in prison. He spent six months in jail because of all of this. I can't tell you how I felt when he was in jail. I can't express it. It is beyond description. When he was in prison, he was beaten and tortured. To get him out of prison, my parents had to pay more money. When he got out of jail the officials told us, *You have committed too many crimes so you have no right to get married*. Then they tore up all of the documents we had submitted to get marriage permission. A friend told me that we could try to pay them more money, but our families had no money left to pay them. So we had to leave."

"This is one way the government tortures us. They don't want the Rohingya population to increase. They say...

'This is not your country.
You don't have the right to reproduce here'."

The parents of this 26-year-old could not afford to continue to pay money to *NaSaKa* to receive permission for her to get married. Unable to marry in Burma, she and her fiancé eventually fled to Bangladesh in 2005.

Noor

Noor and seven other women sit quietly on the floor. They all stare down at the dirt. A bright yellow scarf-like *romal* covers the head and shoulders of one woman, while another is draped in bright green. There is no sound inside the shabby hut. A hot breeze whips through the tattered plastic sheets of the roof a few feet above their heads. The leaves and branches holding the roof in place scratch across the plastic.

"*NaSaKa* asked us, *Where are your husbands?* We told them we didn't know. So they started to pull all of us women out of our houses and made us walk down to the water," Noor says. Some of the women look over at Noor as she tells their story. The others continue to stay focused on the dirt floor.

"First they forced us to walk into the water up to our knees. Then they made us walk out further, where the water went up to our hips. And then they made us walk out until the water went up to our necks. When we were in the water up to our necks the soldiers shouted for us to dunk our heads under water, then come up. Then go under the water again and again. They started throwing mud at us. At the time I was eight months pregnant."

In January 2009, a scuffle occurred between some of the men in Noor's village and local authorities. A month earlier, *NaSaKa* ordered most of the men in Noor's village to provide labor constructing a new border fence between Burma and neighboring Bangladesh. After 30 days of work without pay, the men refused to work any longer. During those 30 days they hadn't been able to provide food for their families or maintain the village shrimp project. The day after the men refused to work, *NaSaKa* returned to the village and destroyed the shrimp project, which then sparked the scuffle. When the men of the village heard that a larger posse of *NaSaKa* planned to return the following day, most fled into the hills. The woman and children of the village stayed. Noor and fifteen other women from the village refused to turn their husbands over.

After the abuse had ended and *NaSaKa* had left, relatives arrived to help the women and take them home. Some were throwing up, others fainted from exhaustion. When they returned home they found their homes had been locked by the authorities. After spending 21 days sleeping in the hills, Noor and the woman were starving and had no choice but to leave. They made their way down to the Naf River like so many had before and hired small canoes to take them to Bangladesh.

"They knew I was eight months pregnant," Noor explains. "They know everything about us. They said, *You are pregnant? We don't care.* We stood in the water for eight hours. They made us look directly into the sun for some of that time. When we were looking into the sun, we were so scared we were crying. We left everything behind."

These women were forced to stand in water up to their necks and were verbally and physically abused by *NaSaKa*. Eventually 120 families from their village fled to Bangladesh.

*"Since birth I have not received human rights.
Our parents did not receive any rights in Burma and
our children will not receive any human rights either.
So, we had to leave and come here to Bangladesh."*

A woman and her grandchild sit on the side of the road at the Tal Makeshift Camp near the town of Teknaf. Most Rohingya in southern Bangladesh are not recognized as refugees and receive little or no humanitarian assistance.

Mohammed

"We first arrived here in Bangladesh in 1948," 65-year-old Mohammed says. "Then we arrived again in 1978, then again in 1991/92. Now people are coming in a sporadic way. I am not satisfied here. All of us hope to return to our motherland. Here, we are staying like prisoners."

A few minutes later, a large horn from a bus screams in the background as it speeds down the two-lane road toward the southern town of Teknaf. Rain has just drenched the camp where Mohammed has lived for the past three years: a narrow 30 meter wide and 800 meter long stretch of swampy marshland between the road and the banks of the Naf River called Tal Camp. Water drains down from the nearby hillside, collecting trash, debris and human waste while sweeping through the camp and through family's huts. Tight walkways and thin spaces in between the primitive huts turn into thick, sludgy, sewage-smelling mud. Nothing escapes the dampness. Everything is wet and everyone looks miserable.

Though 30,000 Rohingya are officially recognized as refugees and reside in two UNHCR monitored refugee camps, this is a fraction of the Rohingya population in Bangladesh. Up to 300,000 Rohingya, like Mohammed, are not provided refugee status, receive little or no humanitarian assistance and live clandestinely throughout southern Bangladesh, working as underpaid day laborers and living a hand-to-mouth existence. Vulnerable, exploited, harassed and frequently the targets of mistreatment and abuse, unrecognized Rohingya time and again have had no choice but to turn to each other for protection, creating makeshift camps for security that ultimately become rife with disease, malnutrition and abject poverty.

Tal Camp was created in response to a Bangladesh government anti-crime operation in 2002 called 'Operation Clean Heart' when thousands of Rohingya were rooted out of local villages in Teknaf. In 2008, conditions for the 10,000 Rohingya living in Tal Camp became so appalling the camp was relocated several kilometers away to Leda Bazar where conditions changed little. That same year, the threat of eviction during a voter registration campaign in Bangladesh displaced thousands more unrecognized Rohingya. Soon, shabby huts were being built along the perimeter of the official refugee camp at Kutupalong. In less than two years, the Kutupalong Makeshift Camp would become home to 34,000 unrecognized Rohingya. What was once empty hills covered in scrub brush, would soon turn into a sprawling maze of squalid shacks made of plastic, mud and leaves, reeking of illiteracy, illness and utter despair.

"Our health is not good here in Bangladesh," Mohammed continues. "Our children are deprived of an education and we have no fundamental rights. In other countries, refugees have rights, but we don't have any. We are trying our best to convince people of our rights but our attempts are in vain. The people here have become more illiterate but the children are the ones who are victimized the most."

Tal Makeshift Camp was created in 2004 in a marshland along the Naf River after Bangladesh authorities launched an eviction campaign in Teknaf. Up to 10,000 Rohingya lived in the camp until it was relocated in 2008.

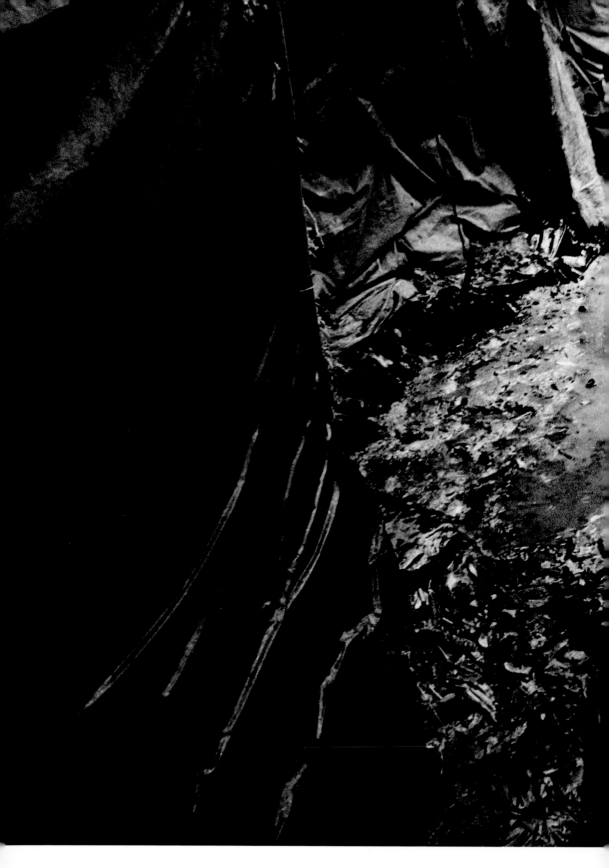

Two children play in a flooded walkway in Tal Camp. During the rainy season, streams of run-off water from the nearby hills mix with open sewers to wash away huts and flood the camp with debris, garbage and human waste.

~

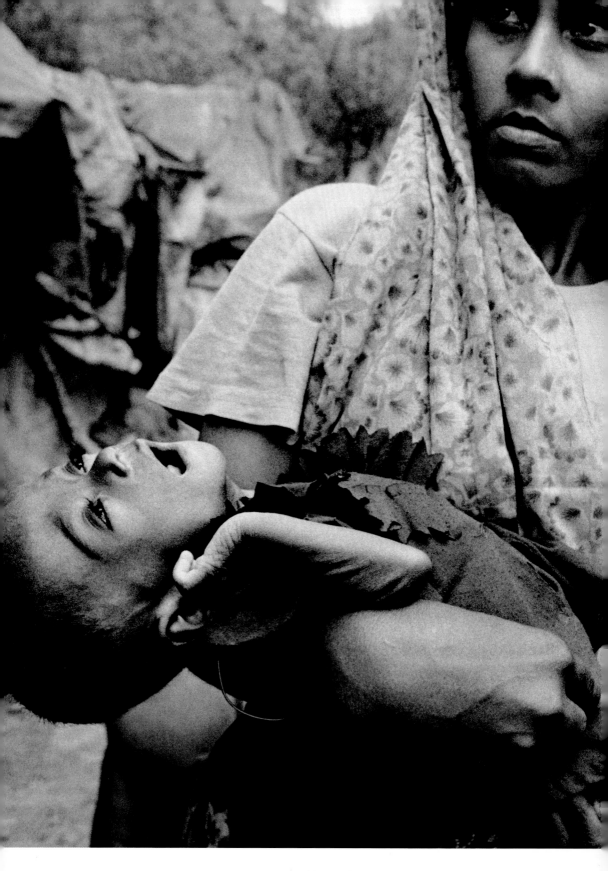

Because of malnutrition, poor sanitation and unclean water, infant mortality in Tal Camp is extremely high. A mother holds her child who has been sick for weeks. One-third of the children in the camp are malnourished.

Local water sources at Tal Camp are contaminated, which has resulted in high cases of water-borne disease. A woman has been sick for over a week and is too weak to stand up. She is unable to receive medical attention.

A group of Rohingya women walk with their children to the town of Teknaf where they will beg for food. Bangladesh authorities arrested their husbands and the women have no way to provide for their children.

Bangladesh considers most Rohingya to be illegal economic migrants. They are unable to work legally, yet they are an important source of labor. Rohingya working in salt fields near Teknaf earn less than $3 USD per day.

Local companies exploit Rohingya for cheaper wages, which has resulted in deeper animosity towards the Rohingya among locals. A Rohingya man breaks apart bricks at a brick factory outside of Teknaf.

"I would like to get rid of my debts but the boat owners of Shamlapur know that if we become free of debt, we would surely leave and find other jobs. So they always increase the amount of debt.

I don't know when and how I will get rid of this debt. Maybe I will have to spend the rest of my life as a bonded laborer."

A group of Rohingya men push their fishing boat back onto shore. Most Rohingya men in the Shamlapur area of Bangladesh work as bonded laborers and are trapped into debt to local Bangladeshi boat owners.

Fish markets like the main fish market in Cox's Bazar rely on Rohingya to do much of the dirty and hard labor, like these two Rohingya men carrying loads of fresh fish to be weighed before being sold.

The coastal area of Naziratek outside of Cox's Bazar is one of the largest fish drying centers in all of Bangladesh. Hundreds of Rohingya workers (mostly women) provide the majority of labor, earning about $1.50 USD per day.

"I was living in a village but there was a problem when the government started asking people for National ID cards. I don't have an ID Card because I am from Burma. When I said that I didn't have an ID Card people in the village told me to leave. So that's when I moved here to Kutupalong where I live in a hut made from things we took from the forest."

In 2008, Rohingya began to create the Kutupalong Makeshift Camp along the outskirts of the official UNHCR monitored refugee camp. What started out as a dozen families is now home to 25,000 Rohingya.

Rohingya hike miles into the forest to collect firewood to sell at local markets or use at the Kutupalong Makeshift Camp. Locals harass the women and police often arrest Rohingya men for taking wood from the forest.

~

Most Rohingya in the Kutupalong Makeshift Camp live in primitive huts made of leaves, twigs, mud and scraps of plastic. The Rohingya in the camp receive little or no humanitarian assistance.

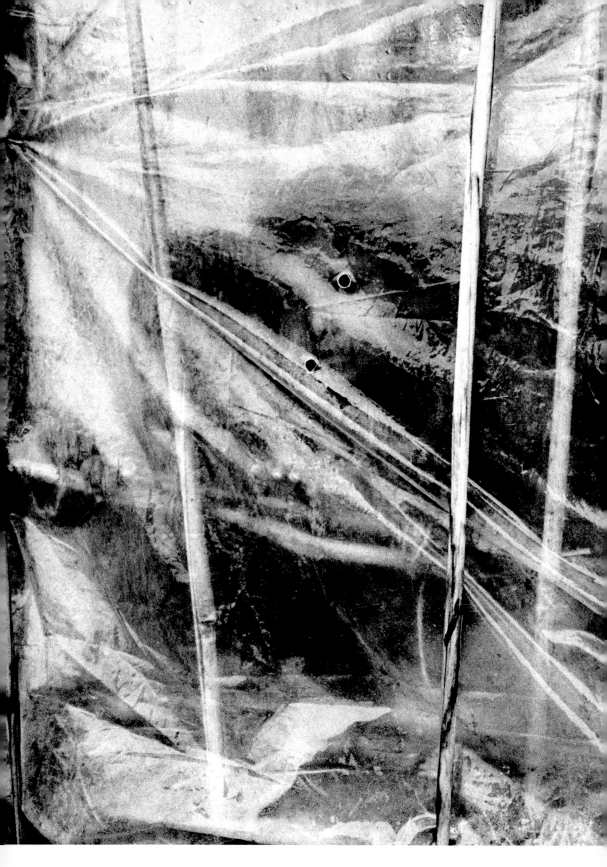

Over 30% of the makeshift camp are children, yet they are not provided an education and have limited access to health care. A group of children attend a makeshift madrassa made of bamboo and plastic sheeting.

"We came to Bangladesh and became refugees. Here we live under plastic sheets. In the daytime it gets very hot. And in nighttime it is very cold. Sometimes at night, dew drops from the plastic sheets of our roof. We are able to work very little and it is not enough to buy food. We eat once but starve twice."

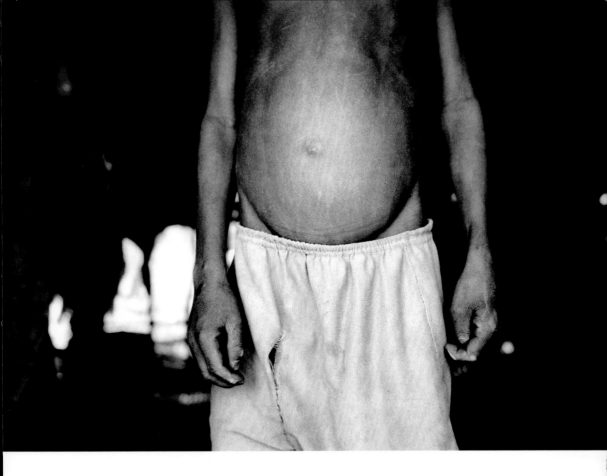

This 30-year-old man broke his leg during forced labor in Burma. He and his family fled to Bangladesh but he has not been able to receive any medical assistance.

This 60-year-old woman has been sick for weeks and has no family members to take care of her. Unable to receive medical assistance she relies on other Rohingya to help her make it from one day to the next.

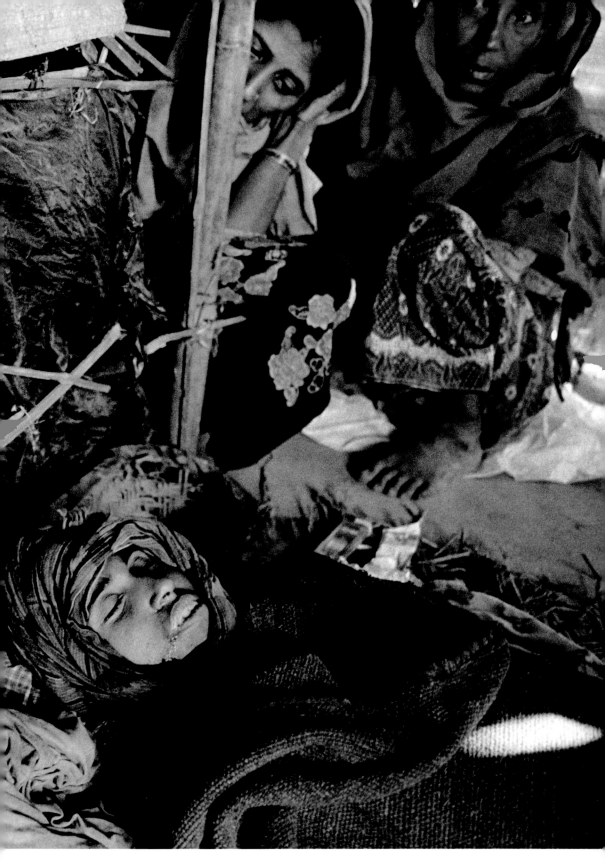

The mother, father and relatives of 15-year-old Sultan Ahmed look over his lifeless body in the Kutupalong Makeshift Camp. He was sick for weeks and died from typhoid on December 20th, 2009.

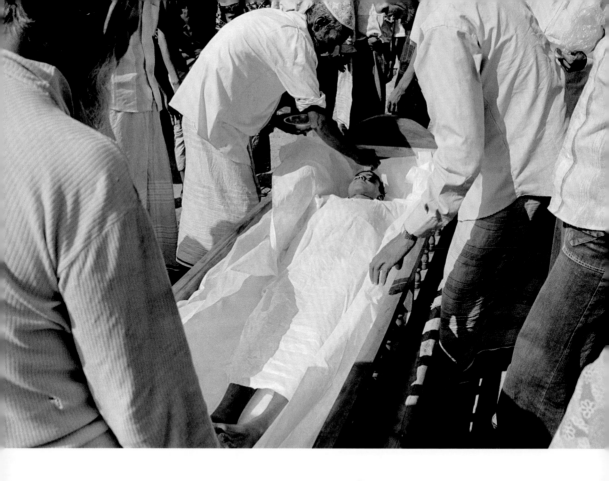

"My son did not have to die like this. He has been sick for weeks.
He was a happy boy. He was a smart boy.

My son was born in Burma without an identity.
Now he has died without an identity here in Bangladesh."

PART THREE

*"There is no life to live here. So he went to find a better one.
He got on a boat two months ago. Now we don't know where he is.
What are his wife and daughters going to do now?"*

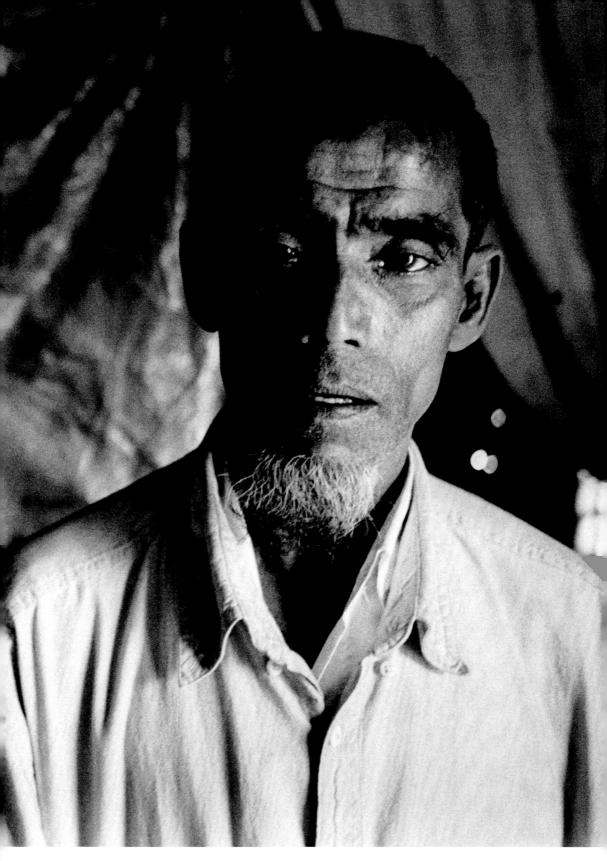

The parents of 27-year-old, Mohammed, have not heard from their son since he got on a boat in early December 2008. He paid a broker 20,000 Taka ($290 USD) to make the journey by boat from Bangladesh to Malaysia.

Jamal

"There were four boats and we all left at the same time," Jamal explains. "My boat left from Teknaf. It had 112 people on it. We left on December 10, 2008. We started at 11pm at night. It was a good boat and we had enough food to last the journey to Malaysia. I paid a broker 30,000 taka (about $435 USD)."

Jamal was 21 years old at the time of his journey to Malaysia. Born in Buthidaung in North Rakhine, he was a day laborer, eking out a living working any agricultural job he could secure, but work became almost impossible to find. Travel restrictions imposed by *NaSaKa* kept Jamal and other Rohingya trapped in their village, unable to travel to find work. Life became a round of no work, no income, and little food. So he left his wife, two children and family behind. When he crossed the Naf River into Bangladesh at the end of 2007, Jamal was certain that he would find enough work to support his family back in Burma. But, as he remembers, "I couldn't find work and the poverty was horrible." That was when he made the decision to travel to Malaysia.

In previous years, thousands of Rohingya had made the clandestine journey, paying smugglers to squeeze them onto rickety and often unseaworthy wooden vessels that would transport them to a place only marginally better than the excruciatingly intolerable life in Burma and the hopeless life in Bangladesh they had left behind. The boat season at the end of 2008 was busy. Brokers throughout the poorest areas of the Cox's Bazar district combed through villages as well as Rohingya makeshift camps on a regular basis seeking out potential customers. Thousands that year agreed to make the journey. The price for the trip was not only an investment in their future but for many Rohingya, it was yet another test as to the lengths they would go to find a way to survive. It was a risk Jamal was willing to take. At the time, he had no idea what lay ahead of him.

"After nine days we reached Thailand," Jamal continues. "We landed on a small beach on an island where we were caught by the Thai authorities.

"We were held by the Thai authorities for several days. They beat us and only gave us one meal every two days. The water they gave us to drink was salty and the food they gave us was mixed with sand. During this time, the Thai authorities caught more people on boats. They caught around 400 Bangladeshi and Rohingya on the boats during this time. Then they loaded all 400 people onto one boat without food and water. There was no engine on the boat. They attached a rope to the boat, took us out to sea and left us.

"We floated around in the middle of the sea for ten days and in those ten days 300 people on the boat died. Most jumped overboard to try to swim. Only one man made it. He jumped overboard and eventually made it to the Andaman Islands. The Indian police captured him. He told them about our boat so they sent people out to try to find us.

"When we were floating in the sea for ten days I thought to myself, *If we are out here for any more days, I am going to die.*"

News of boats filled with emaciated men drifting out at sea in water-filled boats made the international press. Amid harsh criticism, Thailand admitted to the 'pushbacks'. Weeks later, ministers from nations across Southeast Asia met for the annual ASEAN summit meeting with several pushing for a regional solution to the Rohingya 'boat people' situation. But it wouldn't take long for the Rohingya to slip off of the political agenda. Since then, each year, groups of Rohingya men in Burma and Bangladesh continue to embark on the boat journey. Some, the lucky ones, make it to Malaysia. Some are caught by authorities at any number of transit points along the way. Others just disappear, never to be heard from again, leaving only memory and anguish in the minds of the families who wait hoping for a message that never arrives.

From the time of his rescue by Indian authorities, Jamal and dozens of other Rohingya men found drifting at sea in late 2008 and early 2009 have spent years in an Andaman Island jail, living day by day in a state of limbo. Describing his journey via a mobile phone in the prison, Jamal now shares a medium sized room with over 150 other detainees.

"I've been in jail in the Andaman Islands now for three years," Jamal says. "The authorities here don't know what to do with us. They say they have no idea what will happen with us. Two years ago, the Burmese authorities came here and they said to all of us, *You are not coming back to Burma!*

"We just sit here. We have nothing to do. We do nothing all day long. It makes us depressed because we see that we have no future. I don't think I will ever get out because Bangladesh won't take us and Burma won't take us either.

"I'm from Burma but they will shoot me if I return. It is my birth country but I worry about never being able to go back during my life. I dream that one day I will be free and that I will go back to my family. I talked with them six months ago. There is no mobile phone in my village so my wife had to go to another place. We talked and they are not doing well. Now, they are begging in Burma. They are trying to survive."

In Bangladesh, the wife of Imar (40) holds a photo of him in a hospital in Indonesia. Imar got on a boat bound for Malaysia in early December 2008. The boat was intercepted and pushed back out to sea by Thai authorities.

Bangladesh authorities have increased their efforts to stop Rohingya before they get on boats for Malaysia. Caught near Teknaf in the middle of the night, this boat was taking Rohingya to a larger boat waiting out at sea.

A group of Rohingya men are detained at a highway checkpoint in southern Bangladesh. They came to Bangladesh to get on a boat to Malaysia. Bangladesh authorities would push the group back to Burma the same night.

Hafez

The mud walls on the inside of 22-year-old Hafez's hut are smooth and clean. A flower is drawn in chalk on one wall and a baseball cap and clothes hang on another. Seven people live in the small hut, including his nineteen-year-old wife Gul, his young son, his mother-in-law and other extended family. Hafez is the only source of income they have. In Burma, Hafez said, their life had been like torture, constantly interrupted by the fear of what demand *NaSaKa* would create next: a new tax, forced labor, sentry duty. In Bangladesh, they found that life was harsh but at least they could sleep in relative peace at night. But soon this would all change.

"In 2009 I went to Bandarban to work as a farmer," Hafez says. "While I was there, I was arrested by the police. At that time there were five or six Rohingya staying at the house in Bandarban. Some local people informed the police that we were staying at this house.

"It was 1am in the morning. The police came to the house and kicked in the door. They didn't say anything to us. They just took us and put us into the police van. When we were in the van the police asked us, *Where are you from?* We replied, *Satkania, in Chittagong*. We tried to hide where we were from. The police didn't ask us for any documents. We were taken to the police station and stayed there for two nights. They didn't give us food for two days. We tried to escape but the police beat us. After that it was impossible to escape.

"More people were arrested during those two days, over 50 people. All of them were Rohingya living in Bandarban. After two nights they put us into the police van and that night at midnight the police took us to the Burma border and handed us over to the Bangladesh Border Guards (BGB). We were tied together by a strong thick rope. We were all in one line. Fifty people tied up together. There were also women and children too in the line. BGB took us to the border and pushed us across the border back to Burma. When they were pushing us across the border, they were saying, *You are Rohingya. You are Burmese people, so go back to Burma*."

"All of us split into small groups and went into the forest to hide from *NaSaKa*. I have no idea where the women went after they were pushed back into Burma. I don't know where the women fled to. Some probably stayed in Burma. Others probably came back to Bangladesh. We were really scared when we were in Burma. We were scared that we would be found by *NaSaKa*."

In the months following Hafez's arrest at the end of 2009 and beginning of 2010, a wave of fear swept through the Rohingya community in the areas of Cox's Bazar, Ukhia, Bandarban and Teknaf in southern Bangladesh, where local authorities, police and BGB launched a violent crackdown against the Rohingya in these areas. Undocumented Rohingya were pulled off of buses, evicted from where they lived, caught up in raids in villages and arrested where they worked, some even pulled off of the rickshaws they were driving. Anti-Rohingya groups in Teknaf and Ukhia marched in the streets, protesting against the government for not taking a tougher stance on the 'illegal' foreigners. Anti-Rohingya sentiment ran rampant. Announcements over loudspeakers were broadcast in several villages, making threats against Rohingya and warning locals who harbored, housed or employed Rohingya.

As the arrests increased, Rohingya from all over the district flooded into the Kutupalong Makeshift Camp for protection. The camp swelled to over 34,000 people. With little or no access to humanitarian assistance, clean water and sanitation, conditions for those in the camp deteriorated to that of a humanitarian crisis. Families ran out of food because men were too afraid to leave the camp to find work for fear of being arrested. Women whose husbands had been arrested and put in jail found themselves incredibly vulnerable to harassment from locals and struggling to provide for their children. Eventually, the crackdown stopped, but only after thousands of undocumented Rohingya were arrested and forcibly pushed back to Burma. Many like Hafez would return to their families in Bangladesh, but the crackdown would remain with them as just one more reminder of how fragile and defenseless they are in their day-to-day lives.

"I still live with the fear from being arrested. I haven't been back to the Bandarban since then," Hafez says. "I am now scared that I will be caught again. I hear that BGB are catching people again. One of my neighbors was recently captured at one of the checkpoints on the highway and sent back to Burma. He returned to Bangladesh the next day, but I don't want to leave the camp."

After living for years in the Bandarban area of Bangladesh, these two women as well as three other familes were arrested by BGB troops and forcibly sent back to Burma. They eventually returned to Bangladesh.

"One night Bangladesh border troops came to our house, put us in a van and took us to the Burma border. They pushed us back to Burma. When we reached Burma the people there told us that if we were caught, we would be killed. We asked people to show us how to come back to Bangladesh so they did and we came back. At the time, I was holding my baby to my chest. When we got back to Bangladesh, I realized my baby was dead. A hole was dug and I put my baby in it and buried my baby there.

We found a street and signaled for a car to stop and we asked them to take us to a safe place. They told us about Kutupalong Makeshift Camp and brought us here. I had one pair of clothes and gave them to the driver as payment. I have been in Kutupalong for three months. We are alone and many of us are having many problems. We are living in fear that we will be pushed back again. Now we don't have husbands so we are all very afraid. Here we don't have food. I don't have a blanket or a mat and I don't have a door so the wind comes in."

"Now it is winter time and it is cold. No people like us are leading this kind of hard life. Our souls haven't been taken by God, that is why we haven't died yet."

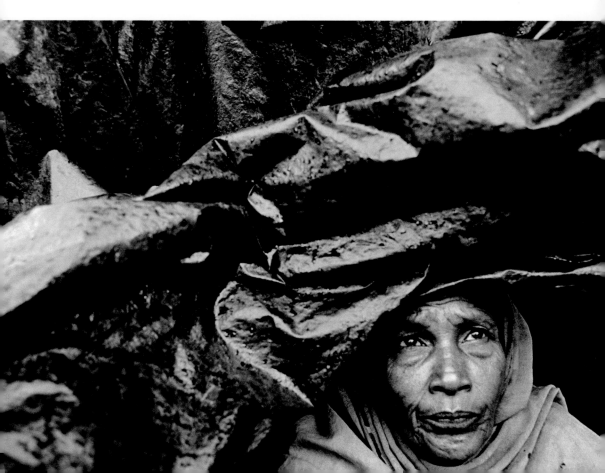

The crackdown against Rohingya in late 2009 displaced thousands of Rohingya. Many like this woman fled to Kutupalong Makeshift Camp for protection. During the crackdown the camp swelled to over 34,000 people.

During the crackdown there was a food crisis in the camp. Unable to buy enough food for her seven children to eat a woman prepares scraps of shrimp that she found on the ground at a market.

"There is a checkpost nearby where they are catching people and arresting them. It's not possible to find work here. I had to travel to Bandarban area to find work. I'd work three days and only make 300-400 taka but much of it was spent on transportation."

"*Everyone is in crisis now. We're not receiving help and no one can borrow from each other.*"

A group of Rohingya is detained after their boat crossed the Naf River and landed in southern Bangladesh. The entire group was pushed back to Burma the same night. Many would return to Bangladesh the next day.

Jubair & Sirajul

A large dark blue bus with bars covering the windows is parked in the cul-de-sac just outside the Cox's Bazar jail in southern Bangladesh. Inside the jail's front door, thirty Rohingya men, old and young, squat in several rows, holding their knees in a cramped space only large enough to fit half of them. All have been recently arrested in a crackdown against Rohingya that has swept across towns and villages in the area. They now join almost 300 other Rohingya men in the jail.

A piece of paper is stuck on the wall behind the jailor's desk. In Bengali it reads, *We Will Protect Them And Let Them See The Light.* "Some have been waiting for a few months, others have been waiting for years," the jailor says. "One man has been waiting for 13 years. He's only 35 years old."

Across the hall, 70-year-old Jubair and two other men, 63-year-old Hassan and 55-year-old Sirajul, walk into the deputy jailor's office. They stand quietly with their backs up against the wall. All three are used to waiting for a long, long time.

A delegation from the Myanmar embassy in Dhaka visits the jail on this day. The men hoped they would finally be released, but in the eyes of the delegation, the men were invisible.

Now seventy years old, Jubair is thin and frail and barely lifts his feet up off of the ground when he walks. He slowly sits down in a wooden chair, rests his hands in his lap and nervously curls his fingers into the well-worn fabric of the sarong-like Burmese *longyi* he's wearing. "I was fishing for Hilsa fish in 1992," he says in a weak, almost inaudible voice. "When I was fishing, my boat got caught in a storm and the current dragged me near Bangladesh. That is when I was arrested by the BDR [Bangladesh Rifles]."

When asked about his sentence, Jubair explains, "I received a two-year sentence in 1992 for illegally crossing the border." Calculations could be seen running through the minds of those in the room. He was arrested in 1992 and given a two year sentence, so his jail term ended in 1994. Today it is 2009 and Jubair is still in prison, 15 years after serving his time.

"God only knows why I've been in here for so long," he says. "Actually, I don't know how long I'll be in here. God only knows."

When it is 55-year-old Sirajul's time to talk, the story is nearly the same: arrested in 1998 and sentenced to two and a half years, he should have been released in late 2000, yet has been sitting in jail nine years too long. Fifteen years younger than Jubair, Sirajul's voice still holds shreds of anger.

"The Burmese government is not taking us. The Bangladesh government knows I am here. The United Nations knows that we are in here. But nothing happens. We just stay in here. I've been in here for a long time and because of that, I've lost my wife, father, mother and children," Sirajul says, and then he stares into nowhere, through the blue painted wall on the other side of the room.

"The problem is that Myanmar doesn't recognize the Rohingya," adds the deputy jailor. He looks at Sirajul and then over at the two other men who are all waiting out their days in limbo with no real hope of change. "What you have to understand is that there are two types of people from Myanmar here in Bangladesh. There are the legal immigrants. They are the ones who are recognized as citizens of Myanmar. And then there are the Rohingya, like these men. And because they do not have citizenship, Myanmar is not going to accept them back." The few people in the room nod in agreement, including Sirajul.

Sirajul stands up from the chair and says softly, "Pray for me."

HISTORICAL TIMELINE

1799

Francis Buchanan publishes *A Comparative Vocabulary of Some of the Languages Spoken in the Burma Empire*. The paper is the first historical document mentioning the *Rooinga*, today's Rohingya. After the fall of the Kingdom of Arakan to Burmese King Bodaw, thousands of Buddhists and Muslims flee Arakan into Chittagong.

1823-4

British invade Arakan during the 1st Anglo-Burma War. The following decades see a large migration of people from the Indian subcontinent into Arakan, mostly Muslims from the Chittagong region. Arakan becomes British Territory in 1826.

1860-1875

Arakanese Buddhists and Muslims who fled to Chittagong during Burmese occupation begin to return to Arakan.

1942

The British retreat as Japanese units enter Arakan, leaving an administration vacuum. Inter-ethnic clashes erupt between Arakanese Buddhists and Muslims. Thousands of Buddhists and Muslims fleeing violence cross over into Chittagong. The clashes split Arakan in an ethnic division that still exists today with South Arakan consisting of mostly Buddhists and North Arakan consisting of mostly Muslim Rohingya.

1947

The Panglong Conference held by Aung San recognizes several ethnic groups to achieve autonomous national states. The Muslim and Buddhist communities from Arakan are not present at the Conference. Aung San is assassinated on July 19, 1947.

1947

The 1947 Constitution of the Union of Burma is proclaimed with some of Burma's first citizenship laws. Muslims from Arakan vote in the 1st Constituent Assembly Elections.

January 4, 1948

The independent Union of Burma is created. U Nu becomes first Prime Minister.

1948

Burma's 1948 Union Citizenship Act is issued. Civil war breaks out across Burma between ethnic groups and the central government, including Arakan, where the Mujahid formed in 1947 push for an Islamic State in North Arakan.

1951

Resident of Burma Registration Act of 1949 is implemented through the 1951 Residents of Burma Registration Rules. National Registration Cards (NRC) are issued. The Rohingya in North Arakan are issued NRCs.

1954

U Nu says the majority of people in Maungdaw and Buthidaung are Rohingya Muslims.

1959

Prime Minister U Ba Sue says the Rohingya are a race like other races in Burma and have equal rights.

1960

Rohingya vote in 1960 Elections.

1961

U Nu creates the Mayu Frontier Administration (MFA), which consists of Maungdaw, Buthidaung and western Rathidaung in North Arakan. The Burma Broadcasting Service (BBS) in Rangoon begins broadcasting a Rohingya Language Program.

1962

General Ne Win overthrows U Nu government in a military coup and sets forth the "Burmese Way to Socialism" which would affect the Rohingya for the next 30 years.

1964

The MFA is eliminated. North Arakan is put under the control of the Ministry of Home Affairs via the administration in Sittwe/Akyab (capital of Arakan).

1965

Broadcasting of the Rohingya Language Program is cancelled.

1974

Burma is renamed the Socialist Republic of the Union of Burma. A new Constitution is adopted. Arakan is renamed and officially becomes the Rakhine State.

1978

Ne Win launches *Operation Naga Min* or 'Operation Dragon King' along the border region. *Naga Min* authorized a sweeping check of identity papers throughout the country in order to purge Burma of illegal foreigners. A wave of terror sweeps over Rakhine, resulting in widespread cases of summary execution, rape and brutality targeted specifically at the Rohingya population. 250,000 Rohingya refugees flood into neighboring Bangladesh.

1979

The international community voices its concern to the United Nations, especially Muslim-country members. Burma and Bangladesh sign an agreement and *Operation Shwe Hintha* (Operation Golden Bird) is launched, assisting nearly all 250,000 Rohingya refugees in their return to Burma

1982

The Ne Win government enacts the 1982 Burma Citizenship Law, with 3 types of citizenship and which in practice provides 'full' citizenship only to those from Burma's 135 recognized 'national races'. The Rohingya are not listed as one of these 'national races'. With the new Citizenship Law, some 800,000 Rohingya in Rakhine State are denied Burmese citizenship, effectively making them stateless.

1988

Pro-democracy demonstrations sweep across Burma. Ne Win resigns. Aung San Suu Kyi emerges as leader of the democracy movement. The State Law and Order Restoration Council (SLORC) take over power in another coup, restoring military rule. Thousands die in a brutal crackdown.

July 1989

Burmese government begins to issue new Citizen Scrutiny Cards to Myanmar nationals throughout the country. Rohingya in North Rakhine were not provided any cards.

1990

SLORC organizes multiparty elections and allow the Rohingya in North Rakhine to vote and create political parties in hopes the Rohingya will side with SLORC. Instead, opposition candidates win majority seats in the Rakhine State. SLORC rejects the results of the vote. Mass demonstrations sweep across the country, including demonstrations in Rakhine.

1991

As a result of demonstrations, SLORC increases military presence in North Rakhine. *Pyi Thaya Operation* or Operation Clean and Beautiful Nation is launched which results in widespread abuse, forced labor, harassment, rape, arbitrary land seizure, destruction of property and executions of Rohingya in North Rakhine. Burma ratifies the UN Convention on the Rights of the Child, which states every child has a right to a nationality.

1991-1992

Over 250,000 Rohingya refugees flood into Bangladesh where twenty refugee camps are created. The UNHCR is not permitted full access to the camps.

1992

Burmese authorities establish the border security/military force *Nay-Sat Kut-kwey Ye* or *NaSaKa* in North Rakhine. *NaSaKa* consists of the police, immigration, customs, military intelligence, and anti-riot police. From 1992 until now, *NaSaKa* would be the main perpetrators of human rights abuses against the Rohingya in North Rakhine.

1992

Burmese and Bangladesh governments sign an agreement to repatriate the 250,000 Rohingya refugees. Bangladesh forcibly returns thousands to Burma. UNHCR withdraws from the return process because Burma does not guarantee enough security for the returnees.

1993

The UNHCR and Bangladesh government sign an agreement so UNHCR can access the refugees. By the time UNHCR monitored repatriation begins, Bangladesh had already forcibly returned some 50,000 Rohingya back to Burma. The UNHCR and the Burmese government sign a Memorandum of Understanding permitting the UNHCR to monitor the repatriation and also to start operating in North Rakhine and in Sittwe.

1994

Hundreds of Rohingya families outside of North Rakhine have their land arbitrarily seized by SLORC authorities and are forcibly resettled to Maungdaw in North Rakhine. Burmese authorities stop issuing birth certificates to Rohingya children.

1994

NaSaKa issues the first local order restricting the marriages of Rohingya in North Rakhine. The order is implemented in North Rakhine and nowhere else in the country. Rohingya in North Rakhine are required to first receive official permission from *NaSaKa* before they marry. Marriage through Islamic law/customs is not recognized. The order is used to humiliate and extort money from Rohingya families. Long delays and denial of permission to marry are common. Failure to obey the order, as well as sexual contact or cohabitation outside of officially authorized marriage, is punishable by fines, prosecution and imprisonment for up to 10 years.

1994-December 1995

230,000 Rohingya have returned to Burma under the repatriation agreement. Burmese authorities start issuing some repatriated Rohingya with Temporary Resident Certificates (TRC) or 'white cards'. The card does not represent Burmese citizenship.

1996-97

Increasing incidents of forced labor, violence, excessive taxation/extortion and travel restrictions force up to 25,000 Rohingya into Bangladesh. Bangladesh denies them refugee status.

1997

Refugees in the Kutupalong camp in Bangladesh protest over being repatriated. SLORC is replaced by the State Peace and Development Council (SPDC).

Feb 2001

Communal riots erupt in Sittwe. Over 20 mosques are destroyed by *NaSaKa*. Travel restrictions are increased against the Rohingya in Rakhine. Since then, travel for Rohingya from North Rakhine to Sittwe is almost completely prohibited.

2002

Bangladesh launches *Operation Clean Heart* to crackdown on crime across the country. Thousands of Rohingya are displaced in an eviction campaign in Teknaf and create the first makeshift camp called Tal Makeshift Camp. In 2004 the camp population was forced to move to a new location along the banks of the Naf River near Teknaf.

2005

NaSaKa issues new local order, requiring all newly married Rohingya couples to sign an agreement to only have two children and requiring Rohingya men to be clean-shaven.

August-October 2007

Thousands of monks and demonstrators protest in Burma's 'Saffron Revolution'. A violent military crackdown quells the protests to international criticism.

2008

Tal Makeshift Camp is relocated to the new Leda Bazar Camp where conditions change little. Bangladesh creates new voter registration list under State of Emergency. Under fear of eviction, many Rohingya families begin to create a new makeshift camp called the Kutupalong Makeshift Camp. In Burma, Rohingya in North Rakhine vote in the constitutional referendum.

December 2008

Several boats containing large groups of Rohingya and Bangladeshi men being smuggled from Bangladesh to Malaysia are detained in Thailand. Thailand begins a new policy of 'pushing back' Rohingya boat people. The boats are towed back out to sea without food, water and engines and left to drift. The boats spend weeks at sea.

Early 2009

Burma begins construction on a new border fence in North Rakhine. Rohingya are used as forced laborers. Boats 'pushed back' by Thai authorities are found drifting near the Andaman Islands and Nicobar. Hundreds have died or gone missing. Burmese Consul-General in Hong Kong, Ye Myint Aung, writes a letter and says the Rohingya were "neither Myanmar People nor Myanmar's ethnic group." He also describes Rohingya people are, "as ugly as ogres."

July 2009

Police and local officials destroy over 250 homes of residents of Kutupalong Makeshift Camp. Bangladesh begins a crackdown against undocumented Rohingya in the Bandarban District. Bangladesh Border Guards (BGB) begin forcibly pushing back Rohingya to Burma. Population of the new Kutupalong Makeshift Camp increases to an estimated 20,000.

October 2009-March 2010

Massive crackdown against unregistered Rohingya refugees in the areas of Cox's Bazar, Ukhia and Teknaf. Local authorities, BGB and anti-Rohingya groups arrest Rohingya, conduct raids where Rohingya work, and evict Rohingya from where they live. Anti-Rohingya groups march in the streets of Ukhia and Teknaf and make announcements and threats over loudspeakers against Rohingya.

February 2010

Undocumented Rohingya flood into the Kutupalong Makeshift Camp for protection The population of the camp swells to 34,000 people. By the time the crackdown ends, several thousand Rohingya have been arrested and pushed back to Burma.

May 2011

Under a UN Joint Initiative, the European Commission offer Bangladesh a grant of $33 million USD to reduce poverty in Teknaf and Ukhia sub-district in Cox's Bazar District, where the majority of unrecognized Rohingya refugees live in Bangladesh. Bangladesh refuses the grant saying it would only encourage more Rohingya in Burma to settle in Bangladesh.

September 2011

Bangladesh and Burma agree on the repatriation of about 2,500 Rohingya refugees from the camps following Bangladesh Prime Minister Sheikh Hasina's visit to Burma.

September 2011

Exclusion of the Rohingya and policies of restriction reaffirmed in Parliament by the new government in Burma.

2012

The two official refugee camps Kutupalong and Nayapara created in 1991 continue to hold 30,000 official refugees. Estimates say some 200,000—400,000 stateless, unrecognized Rohingya now live in southern Bangladesh, including 20,000 in the Kutupalong Makeshift Camp and 10,000 in Leda Bazar settlement.

BIOGRAPHIES

Greg Constantine

Greg Constantine was born in the United States and moved to Asia in late 2005. For the past six years he has worked on one, long-term project titled *Nowhere People*, which documents the struggles of stateless minority groups around the world. His work has received awards in Pictures of the Year International (POYi), NPPA Best of Photojournalism, Days Japan, the Human Rights Press Awards in Hong Kong, the SOPA Award from the Society of Publishers in Asia and in 2011 was shortlisted for the Amnesty International Media Award for Photojournalism in the UK. He was also part of a team of journalists from the *International Herald Tribune* awarded the annual Osborn Elliott Prize for Journalism in Asia by the Asia Society.

He is a recipient of a visiting research fellowship from Oxford Brookes University in the UK (2008), an OSI Distribution Grant from the Documentary Photography Project of the Open Society Institute (2009) and a project grant from the Pulitzer Center on Crisis Reporting (2012). Exhibitions and projections of his work have been held in Dhaka, London, Geneva, Madrid, Nairobi, Los Angeles, Hong Kong, Manila, Bangkok, Belgrade, Washington DC and the United Nations Headquarters in New York City. In 2011, he was selected by the Open Society Foundation to participate in the group exhibition, Moving Walls 19. Constantine's first book, *Kenya's Nubians: Then & Now* was released in November 2011. He is currently based in Southeast Asia.

Emma Larkin

Emma Larkin is the pseudonym of an American writer who was born, raised and still lives in Asia. She studied the Burmese language at the School of Oriental and African Studies in London and is the author of *Finding George Orwell in Burma* (Penguin, US, 2005). Larkin has been visiting Burma for over 15 years and her most recent book, *Everything is Broken* (Granta, UK, 2010, also titled *No Bad News for the King*, Penguin, US, 2010), about the catastrophic aftermath of Cyclone Nargis in Burma, was shortlisted for the 2011 Helen Bernstein Book Award for Excellence in Journalism.

ACKNOWLEDGEMENTS

This book is dedicated to the countless Rohingya who have shared such personal stories and moments with me over the past six years.

To Chris Lewa and the Arakan Project for the amazing work you do and for all of your time, guidance and enthusiasm throughout this entire project.

To Saleem, Hannan, Asad, Shahidul, Kajal, Russell, Mohi and many others in Cox's Bazar. I'll always be indebted to you for your eyes and ears, for all of your hard work and your generous hospitality.

To I.U. Bayzid for your advice, resourcefulness and abundant knowledge, but most of all, for your friendship these past six years.

Special thanks to Philip McClellan, Tala Skari, Mark McDonald, Anny Li and many others at the *International Herald Tribune* in Hong Kong and Paris for years of support and for seeing the importance of this work and exposing it to your readers. To the editors at the *Irrawaddy Magazine*, the *New York Times* and *DATUM Magazine*.

Additional thanks go to: Jim Worrall, Lynn Yoshikawa, Joel Charny, Maureen Aung-Thwin and many others at OSI, Amal DeChickera, Kitty McKinsey, the statelessness unit of the UNHCR, Amnesty International Hong Kong, Ryan and Matt at Documentary Arts Asia, Yumi Goto, Mark and his team at BLOOM, Brad Blitz and Maureen Lynch for helping to open doors and for always believing in a way for me to continue this work, to Seth Mydans and Mariko Takayasu, Roland Neveu, Helen Kudrich Coleman, Liz Smailes and many others whose names I have not mentioned.

To Dawn Calabia, Melanie Teff, Sarnata Reynolds and Refugees International for helping to make this book possible. To the Pulitzer Center on Crisis Reporting for providing the final support I needed to complete my work.

Many thanks go to those who looked at early drafts and whose suggestions and feedback made this into a much better book, including: Nic Dunlop, Yvan Cohen, John McDermott, Ben Davies, Billy Sprague, Eric Paulsen and Narisara.

To Emma Larkin, Tomás Ojea Quintana, David Mathieson, Michel Gabaudan, Harn Yawnghwe, Benjamin Zawacki, António Guterres and Aryeh Neier for believing in the importance of the Rohingya story and for contributing such insightful perspectives to this book.

My deepest gratitude to Gina, Joe, Chris, Naomi, Veronique, Jason, Peter and Paul. My appreciation for your trust, support of my work and vision for it goes beyond words.

To my mother and father for your endless optimism that things can change. And to my brother for your eye for detail and for always listening.

Most of all, to Jennifer. For tolerating my long and frequent absences away from home, for believing in my work as much as I do, for always pointing me in the right direction and for your trust and love.

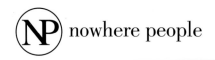

nowhere people

Exiled To Nowhere: Burma's Rohingya is the second book from the project *Nowhere People*. The *Nowhere People* book series intends to highlight the plight of stateless people around the world and increase awareness of the issue of statelessness. The first book in the series, *Kenya's Nubians: Then & Now* was published in November 2011.

www.exiledtonowhere.com
www.nowherepeople.org

Photographs for this book were taken over the course of eight trips to Bangladesh from 2006-2012. Reporting for this project was supported in part by grants from Kingston University, UK (Sept 2010) and the Pulitzer Center on Crisis Reporting (Feb 2012).

Publication of this book was supported in part by funding from Refugees International.

REFUGEES INTERNATIONAL

Exiled To Nowhere: Burma's Rohingya © 2012 Greg Constantine

Photographs © Greg Constantine
Foreword © Emma Larkin
All other text by Greg Constantine
Small photograph on pages 128-129 © and courtesy of Hotli Simanjuntak
Map © David Lindroth Inc.
Quote on page 79 courtesy of The Arakan Project

Design by Greg Constantine & Helen Kudrich Coleman
Cover image retouching: Steven Coleman
Production Consultant: Roland Neveu
Text Editor: Liz Smailes

All Rights Reserved. No part of this publication many be reprinted, reproduced or transmitted in any form or by any means, electronic or mechanical, including photocopy, recording or any other information storage system now known or hereafter invented with out prior permission in writing from Greg Constantine.

First edition, 2012
ISBN 978-0-9838346-1-8
Printed in Thailand